Principles of
Perfect Leadership

Sri Dharma Pravartaka Acharya

Nayaka Tattva Sutras

Principles of Perfect Leadership

Sri Dharma Pravartaka Acharya

ISDS
Omaha, NE, USA
2022

International Sanatana Dharma Society
13917 P Street
Omaha, NE 68137

© Copyright 2022, Dharma Ascending Press

www.dharmacentral.com

Table of Contents

More so than any other single attributive factor, you know a true leader by the degree of his or her personal character and integrity. The greatest leader has the greatest depth of character. A so-called leader who is lacking in character is not a leader at all. That deep and abiding character, in turn, must be attributable to the leader's total reliance upon the wisdom and guidance of the ancient ways. The leader's world-view, leadership style and personal behavior must be a reflection of the eternal traditional ways. It is in fidelity to eternal Dharma that true character is rooted.

- Sri Dharma Pravartaka Acharya

Other Works by Sri Dharma Pravartaka Acharya

Introduction to Sanatana Dharma

Sanatana Dharma: The Eternal Natural Way

The Sanatana Dharma Study Guide

The Dharma Manifesto

The Vedic Way of Knowing God

Living Dharma

Radical Universalism: Are All Religions the Same?

Taking Refuge in Dharma

The Shakti Principle

Principles of Perfect Leadership

Interregnum

Be Strong

Lord of the Rings, Dharma and Modernity

The Vedic Encyclopedia

Vedanta: The Culmination of Wisdom

Jnana Yoga: The Art of Wisdom

The Dharma Dialogues

Audio

Mantra Meditations (CD)

All these works can be purchased at: Dharmacentral.com

Sri Dharma Pravartaka Acharya

Dedication

This book is dedicated to my many sincere and dedicated students and disciples currently situated in over seventy nations (and rapidly growing) throughout the length and breadth of the world. Many of my students are destined to eventually become precisely the sort of true leaders written about in the pages of this book. I am aware that many of my students will be called upon in the near future to humbly come forward as the empowered leaders of the coming Golden Age. May God bless and keep safe these future leaders of their respective Dharma Nations.

Aum Tat Sat

Introduction

The beginning decades of the 21st century have been an era during which we have witnessed the proverbial perfect storm of multiple crises all hitting us at once. These numerous challenging events that we have experienced have included political, social, economic, cultural, religious, and health (including individual and pandemic) crises – both large and small – the likes of which have not been attested to in previous history. These many problems have been catastrophically debilitating in myriad ways, very often leading to ill-health, poverty, anxiety, a deep sense of hopelessness and depression, injustice, dwindling faith in the spiritual, and overall suffering for untold hundreds of millions of people throughout the earth. The actual root foundation of our world's compounded crises, however, has not actually originated from any one of these specific areas of concern themselves.

Rather, the very root of the many peripheral problems of our era has arisen solely and directly from a severe crisis of leadership. We have been lacking true leaders for several generations now. When there is a severe vacuum in good leadership, fraudulent and corrupt "leaders" will swiftly maneuver themselves to fill that vacuum. With such parasitic individuals temporarily occupying the seats of true leaders, positive and beneficial change in society then becomes an impossibility. This is the case because meaningful and fundamental change in society tends to take place from the top, and not from the bottom, echelons of society.

Meaningful societal change is very rarely, if ever, significantly addressed or effectuated from the bottom up. Qualitative change for the better rarely comes from the high-pitched, angry voices of the general masses. Rather, meaningful change has always occurred from the top on down, from the level of true and able leadership. One good and highly qualified leader has the ability to radically change the world for the better much more so than even a million ordinary folk. It is true leaders who have the ability to change the course of world history.

Unfortunately, we are currently experiencing a crisis of leadership the likes of which has never been experienced in modern human history. This present crisis of leadership stems back to at least the ending of the Second World War, if not arguably even a bit earlier. Truly authentic leaders are more difficult to recognize and find today than at any other time in recent human history. When we examine the current crop of political, religious, academic or cultural leaders, more often than not what we witness is rampant corruption, mediocrity, self-service and outright stupidity in most modern pretenders to leadership, rather than leaders who are truly qualified and possessed of a good heart. Most of our so-called leaders today are more akin to grifters than great men.

Over the last several generations, we have been given many reasons to lose faith completely in the vast majority of our existing leaders. Whether it is fraudulent spiritual teachers and religious leaders grifting their way to wealth and fame at the expense of their congregations; or duplicitous political leaders reveling in the criminal gains of their own unbridled corruption and hunger for power at the direct expense of their trusting constituents; or deceitful mainstream news anchors, news producers, and journalistic kingpins purposefully forcing propaganda upon their innocent viewers and readers; or debauched and narcissistic celebrities within the entertainment industry killing our culture one woke movie or politically correct TV show at a time – the people have now grown beyond weary of being lied to and being purposefully led down wrong paths by fake leaders. The people are crying out for true leaders to arise once again!

"Where have all of our true and legitimate leaders gone?" is the collective, exasperated question that we now hear from so many suffering and dejected people today. We have been severely lacking the stabilizing, guiding and reassuring presence of strong, honest and authentic leaders that so many previous generations seemingly took for granted. Even though it may sometimes seem as if we should just give up on the very idea of ever again witnessing true leaders arise amongst us, however, true leaders are destined to arise again.

Despite the severe lack of many true leaders today, there have been a small handful of leaders who have arisen in the last decade who are actually authentic, highly capable, and who possess deep integrity. There are now a growing number of leaders who sincerely care for the well-being of the people they represent, and who are leading with honor. Even with the present arising of true leaders, however, the question still remains of how we are to be equipped with the ability to tell the difference between true versus untrue leaders.

The purpose of *Principles of Perfect Leadership* is precisely to explain, in unambiguous and authoritative detail, what a true leader is and what a true leader is not. The criteria that are used to gauge whether or not a person is a true leader are several. These include first and foremost the teachings on leadership and many examples of incomparable leaders that are contained in the Vedic literature, the most ancient body of literature known to humanity, and the scriptural source of the tradition of Sanatana Dharma (The Eternal Natural Way). Another measure that is used to determine what is a true leader are the examples of such leaders throughout history, as well as the writings of the Classical philosophers upon the subject of leadership. The final criteria consists of my own decades of experience in having personally trained many hundreds of my students to fulfill the role of leaders in the service of God and the world. As the number of such true leaders continues to rise, we must all extend our own, personal support to them.

We need to support Dharma by actively encouraging those authentic leaders of the Vedic community (and of our nations generally) who are themselves supporting Dharma. The support of such leaders needs to be practical and immediate. Without hesitation, we need to donate funds, to volunteer with any skills or talents that we have, and to help spread the teachings of such authentic leaders to the entirety of the world. We also need to transform ourselves, with the direct empowerment and guidance of pure and authentic *gurus*, to ourselves become able and authentic leaders of the Vedic community.

Principles of Perfect Leadership is a book that is authoritatively designed to help guide you in recognizing who is - and who is not - a true leader, and in potentially becoming just such a true leader yourself. This book has been written and designed in the style of the ancient literary genre known as the *Sutra* literature. The traditional *Sutra* literature is an important, and highly philosophically oriented, subgenre of the general corpus known as the Vedic literature. Whether we are referring to the *Yoga Sutras*, the *Brahma Sutras*, the *Nyaya Sutras*, the *Narada*

Bhakti Sutras, or any other component of the esoteric *Sutra* literature, all *Sutra* works must rigidly conform to a strict set of formulaic criteria in order be accepted as a legitimate part of the *Sutra* body of works.

Even though *Principles of Perfect Leadership* is written in the English language, rather than the traditional Sanskrit that all ancient *Sutras* were written in, this present work has been written to serve as a modern-day *Sutra* in every important manner. It thus strictly conforms in all essential ways to the literary structural form and the historically attested mood of all previously written *Sutra* works.

In keeping with the *Sutra* tradition, the very first aphorism of this book challenges the reader with the task at hand: to now embark upon the journey of understanding the nature of true leadership. The last aphorism, likewise, offers the necessary postscript of the work just read. As is an essential element of all traditional *Sutra* works, I lay out in the beginning of the work the epistemic mechanisms (*pramanas*) that I as the author accept both as valid and as operational in the delivery of the knowledge contained in the *Sutra*. Also in keeping with the *Sutra* tradition, this book consists of a logically sequential string of powerful aphorisms (*sutras*) designed to deliver to the reader the very art and science of true leadership. Each of the five chapters are also organized in the tradition *Sutra* fashion, and are thus called *adhyayas* (chapters). *Principles of Perfect Leadership* uses an ancient literary form in order to convey its truths in the most modern of language for today's audience. Thus, *Principles of Perfect Leadership* represents the very first instance of a legitimate *Sutra* work revealed in the historical context of modernity.

Each of the aphorisms contained in *Principles of Perfect Leadership* communicates the condensed wisdom of the ancients. It is meant to be read slowly and with patience. Each aphorism should be meditated upon and contemplated with openness of mind and steadfastness of purpose. If you can fully comprehend each and every one of the aphorisms contained in this book, you will know fully and authoritatively what it means to be a true leader.

Aum Tat Sat

Dharma-Pravartaka Acharya
President-Acharya
International Sanatana Dharma Society
Dharmacentral.com

Acknowledgements

I wish to offer my sincere thanks to Nick Kubash for creating the wonderful cover design for this book. His portfolio can be found at: www.artstation.com/nickkubash. I wish to thank Tulasi Devi Mandaleshvari for helping to proofread and format this work for publication. Thank you to Brittnee Hughes for her wonderful graphic design assistance. I also offer my gratitude to Vaidya Savitri Devi for her valuable assistance in proofreading and formatting this book.

Adhyaya One: Basics of Leadership

1.1 Now, then, is the time to inquire into the nature of perfect leadership.

1.2 A perfect leader is non-distinct in his essential nature from the Spirit of his people. He personifies the very best of his people in every and all respects. He and his people are forever united as one. He is an individual who manifests in his unique personality the highest aspirations of his people, and who actively inspires and guides his people in the achievement of those lofty aspirations. He represents the very best of what his people are and can be. When a distinct group, people or nation is blessed with such a rare leader, they are manifestly assured of achieving all positive attainments, victories and prosperities. But being devoid of such a true leader, the people are at the mercy of terrible evil.

1.3 The three valid epistemic sources of knowledge by which we discern the nature of leadership, and through which we judge any information about the art of leadership, are through the means of a) *pratyaksha* (observational, empirical and sensory evidence), b) *anumana* (reason, logic and inference) and c) *shabda* (the divine words of the Vedic scriptures and of the liberated sages). Knowledge concerning leadership should conform to these three epistemic means. If such knowledge does not conform to one or another of these three epistemic mechanisms, then it should be rejected as invalid.

1.4 The practical means by which we learn the nature of leadership are: a) by the didactic examples, innate characteristics and words of great leaders in the past, b) by the words and example of the Acharya (spiritual preceptor) and of the divine monarch, and c) by the teachings of the Vedic scriptures (*Shastra*). Knowledge concerning leadership must conform to these three sources of valid teachings. If such knowledge does not conform to these three sources of valid teachings, then such information should be rejected as invalid.

1.5 The art of leadership includes perfectly understanding and actively pursuing the nature, characteristics, skills, behavior and mindset of outstanding leaders found throughout history. It also often includes pursuing similar strategies as these great past heroes. Diligently study the words, actions, behavior and deeds of previous good leaders found in history. A present day leader is the contemporary manifestation of those among his ancestors who were also great leaders.

1.6 One cannot be a leader unless his foundation is rooted firmly in the past glory of previous leaders, while his goals simultaneously stretch forward to a glorious future for his people. His heart must be situated in the ancient, in the realm of his ancestors; but his vision must be focused on the future.

1.7 Always maintain deep wariness and apprehension about any concocted information on the nature of leadership that is offered by the natural enemy of your people. Your enemy always wishes your demise, and not your success. The advice that is provided to you by your enemy must be treated as a deadly poison unless conclusively proven otherwise.

1.8 Being a manager is not necessarily synonymous with being a leader. A manager gets things done on a day to day basis. He is a person of practical, hands-on action. He leads a team to achieve a smaller and shorter term goal. A leader, on the other hand, focuses on much larger and longer term goals. He is a person of vision who inspires his people to make that vision manifest. A leader is the personification of the righteous goal. A truly accomplished leader, however, is both a person of vision, as well as someone who can also get things done in a practical manner. While a manager cannot always aspire to be a great leader in the broader sense, a leader must always possess excellent management skills.

1.9 A leader fully knows and embraces his true identity. His true identity is present in every layer of his personhood. He has a clear understanding and pride in his spiritual, religious, national, genetic and ethnic identity, as well as in his identity as a man. If a person does not possess the courage and integrity to even be clear on the fundamental facts of what he is and of what he is not, then he does not possess the ability to be clear on any matters of importance. A true leader knows who he is and does not ever shy away from that intrinsic identity.

1.10 Only a specific and genetically exclusive ethnic group can constitute the basis of what is termed a people. Each distinct people represents a singularly unique and non-replicable folk assemblage, all of whom share in the same immutable genetic characteristics. It is this one indigenous and autochthonous people who, in turn, form the whole of the population of the nation proper. There has never been, currently is no such entity, and never shall be a multicultural or a multi-ethnic national state in any intellectually or politically meaningful sense. A true nation is not merely a specific geographic location demarcated by agreed upon borders, or an artificially designated economic zone, or a state predicated merely upon a mutually accepted charter of guiding political principles. A nation is comprised of a specific ethnic people,

and that represents that one specific ethnic people exclusively. An actual nation represents one, and only one, distinct ethnic people. A true nation is by definition exclusive in its nature, not inclusive of those who are not homogenous with the indigenous population.

1.11 A true leader represents only his own people, specifically and exclusively. A true leader must have a healthy sense of pride, communion and fidelity only toward his own people, his own nation, and his own ethnic folk. Anyone who is either ashamed of his own ethnic folk, or who works actively against the best interests of his own people, is nothing less than a deadly enemy of his own people. He is a traitor to his own people. By definition, such a fraud is at odds with the very people who he claims to lead. Thus, he is a poison within the social body. Such a venal individual is an imposter - not a leader - and deserves to be thoroughly exposed and rejected by his people as their very worst enemy.

1.12 A person who fully exhibits both the practical and the intellectual attributes of leadership is necessarily someone who knows the art of being an effective leader. This is why such a person who is possessed of both action and wisdom will always be successful, while others who are lacking the possession of both the ability to act and the wisdom to discern will continue to only dream of success, but never achieve it.

1.13 No two individual human persons are equal, identical, or the same in any manner of significance. Equity of human personhood is a delusion and a lie. Some persons are clearly superior to others in their essential characteristics, inherent attributes, and chosen behavior, while others are clearly inferior in all of these same areas. Many of the remainder of individual persons are simply mediocre and average in what they are, in what they aspire toward, and in what they are reasonably capable of doing and achieving. The true and authentic leader, on the other hand, is a superior person in most, if not all, respects due to possessing both the inherent and acquired merits in his personality that signal superiority, and thus natural authority.

1.14 We know what is superior and what is inferior by knowing the principles of Dharma perfectly. It is in understanding Dharma perfectly that the natural and organic subtleties of reciprocal hierarchical interplay are revealed to us. If you wish to be a leader, then always strive unapologetically and without any hesitation to be superior in everything that you are, in everything that you aspire toward, and in everything that you do. Be superior always in all of your thoughts, words and actions.

1.15 *Principles of Perfect Leadership* has been written for the purpose of explaining the art of leadership in accordance with the teachings of Sanatana Dharma, the eternal natural way. It is written for that person with true leadership potential who is willing to fully manifest his innate talents of a) ability of action and b) wisdom of discernment. If one perfectly studies and applies the teachings of the *Principles of Perfect Leadership* in his own life under the tutelage of an authentic *guru*, and in accordance with the principles of Dharma, he will - in time - become a true and perfect leader.

Adhyaya Two: The Qualities of a Leader

2.1 Sanatana Dharma is not a path of sheep, but of lions. A leader models himself upon the example of the lion. Like the lion, a leader is regal, strong, majestic, and dignified. Like the lion, a leader is courageous, fierce, and protective when a given situation warrants such characteristics. It is toward the true leader that his tribe, people or nation look for protection, encouragement and direction. Sanatana Dharma demands of us that we thoroughly reject any form of weakness, passivity, cowardice or effeminacy. Sanatana Dharma teaches us how to be like the greatest of lions.

2.2 The most important personality trait of a leader is *dhira*, or gravitas. A leader possesses the seriousness in attitude, the stability in personality, and the self-possessed restraint of the mightiest mountain. A true leader only smiles when the situation calls for it, does not constantly joke with others, does not engage in petty quarrels with detractors, or debate endlessly the merits of his vision. The leader is like unto a tremendous mountain, the firmness of which is unquestionable. When you observe the gravitas of a leader, it is as if you are witnessing the presence of a human mountain. The leader is unmovable by any force in creation, with the exception of doing that which sustains Dharma.

2.3 A true leader understands that his personal appearance and aesthetic presentation is a direct reflection upon his people and his mission. He understands that his personal aesthetic profile is yet another tool by which he affects the results that he wishes to accomplish in his mission. He, thus, takes a very healthy pride in every aspect of his appearance. He instinctively presents his personal appearance in the very best, most impressive, and most positive light at all times, regardless of the situational circumstances that he finds himself in. He always dresses impeccably from head to toe, and he has his own unique and signature style. He never presents himself in a low class, vulgar or tasteless manner. He is usually the best dressed man in any room. He is always well-groomed; his hair and beard are never unkempt.

He does not curse; is never crass; does not engage in trivial conversations; and is always neat, clean and fresh in appearance. His outward appearance perfectly reflects his inner stature.

2.4 Understanding that etiquette is nothing less than the social application of the sacred principles of ethics and morality, the true leader always observes the strictest degree of etiquette, manners and gentlemanliness toward all good people who he encounters. He is always a perfect gentleman in all of his interactions with good people. He treats all good people with respect, courteousness, and charity. The only individuals toward whom the leader may choose to not apply the rules of etiquette are toward those who are evil, and toward the enemies of his people. Even toward such adversaries, however, rescinding the rules of etiquette should only be done as an absolutely last resort, and only if it will give the leader an advantageous position to help his people that cannot otherwise be gained by other means.

Good manners toward good people is not optional for the true leader. Rather, his good manners are a reflection of his good inner self.

2.5 A true leader observes a disciplined and daily practice of meditation. A true leader has a strong, disciplined and focused mind. His mind is as sharp as the steel of a powerful sword. If a person is incapable of sitting still in the disciplined silence of meditation, with deep contentment, for a significant duration of time, then that person is not qualified to be considered a true leader. A true leader is nothing less than a master of meditation.

2.6

(i) What it means to be a fully true man is to fully know your true self.

(ii) It is only via the discipline of meditation that you can fully know your true self.

(iii) Therefore, fully true men are only those men who engage in the discipline of meditation.

2.7 A leader is known by his ability to maintain silence, contented inwardness, and complete control over his speech. He never speaks frivolously or displays his inner thoughts and emotions for the world to observe. He controls with exact precision what he communicates to the world in his speech and in his personal actions, and what he does not communicate. He knows what to say, when to say it, and to whom he should say it. He only offers as much information as is absolutely necessary to achieve his immediate and long-term goals. One who cannot control the urges of his tongue perfectly can never be an effective leader.

2.8 A wise leader has complete control over his emotions and mental faculties. He never allows those around him to know his inner emotional or mental state. His feelings and thoughts remain a mystery to those who approach him. He keeps his feelings and his thoughts exclusively to himself, only sharing a fraction of his feelings and thoughts with those from whom he is actively seeking trusted advice. One who feels the constant need to express his feelings can never hope to be a leader. Only a child, a woefully failed adult, or someone with nothing of any real value to accomplish in this world expresses his emotions and thoughts too freely.

2.9 A leader can be addicted to nothing. He must be in supreme control over all of his faculties at all times if he wishes to be truly effective and successful in the pursuit of his goals. Drunkenness, intoxication and addictions to anything clouds a person's judgement, warps his perceptions, debilitates his emotional maturity, makes it difficult for him to distinguish fantasy from reality, makes him dependent upon something that is a foreign imposition upon his true self, and poisons his inner world. For these reasons, a true leader must avoid all narcotics (including all cannabis, ayahuasca, etc.), alcohol, tobacco and all other unnatural addictions, such as video games, pornography, etc. It is only by having a clear mind, sharp vision, and an unalterable connection with reality that a leader can lead with precision.

2.10 The time that a leader has been afforded is an invaluable resource. He cannot afford to waste it. He does not waste his time with irrelevant and selfish, low-class pursuits. A leader does not engage in such wasteful activities as going to bars, watching sports, gossiping, pursuing trivial entertainment, or playing video games. He always spends his spare time in learning and growing intellectually, becoming healthier and stronger, being deeply steeped in meditation, enjoying rejuvenating and healthy rest, and growing in every dimension of his personal being. A leader who is not always improving himself with the time given to him is a leader who is neither dynamic nor wise.

2.11 Fervor toward a goal or desired object becomes manifest as one of three distinct qualitative types, each corresponding to one of the three *gunas* (modes of material energy). Being addicted to a goal or object is of the nature of *tamas*, or ignorance. Addiction is never a positive state, and is to be avoided at all times by those who are wise. Being obsessed with a goal or object is of the nature of *rajas*, or uncontrolled passion. Obsession can be a powerful motivator in achieving material ends; but it is also dangerously bordering upon addiction. With obsession, one becomes the hapless slave of his goal. Being determined to achieve a goal or object that is deemed to be a positive good is of the nature of *sattva*, or purity and goodness. Determination must always be cultivated by anyone who

wishes to achieve unequivocal success in any right-eous pursuit, either material or spiritual. Let sattvic determination fuel your quest for both abundance and spiritual liberation.

2.12 One of the definitions of leadership is to always make your followers feel that they have to work hard in order to keep up with you. Being a leader means that you will work harder, better, and with more energy and enthusiasm toward your goal than any of your followers will. It is in witnessing and marveling in your hard work and zeal that your followers will be inspired to give their maximal effort toward achieving the goal you have set forth for them. If you are unprepared or unwilling to work very hard, with maximal energy, then you are not prepared to be a true leader.

2.13 What is the mark of a true leader? A true leader is the very first person in the room to proclaim with confident humility that "I'll take care of it", and upon hearing him say this, everyone else in that room has zero doubt that the task will now be accomplished. When he does delegate tasks to others, he does so expertly, understanding fully the nature of both the task at hand and the nature of the person to whom he will assign that task. A true leader is decisively unhesitant in his actions and he fully inspires confidence in others.

2.14 In his own mind, a true leader never truly loses a battle. He either wins the battle, or else he learns and grows from his mistakes on the field of battle. He never gives in to despair or self-pity in the face of supposed failure. Rather, he makes sure that he never replicates his previous mistakes in the future. He gives his all to make sure that he has nothing less than victory in subsequent battles. In this way, he actually wins with each battle spiritually - and he eventually wins the war itself.

2.15 It is unmanly to be forced to apologize for one's truthful words or virtuous deeds that were performed in the service of one's goal. To apologize diminishes the leader's stature in the eyes of others and disempowers him personally. A leader never apologizes for any of the statements or actions that he was responsible for during the course of his leadership. A leader is always unapologetic under such circumstances. This is especially the case because he never should have committed any improper statements or actions in the first place.

2.16 Both qualified men, as well as qualified women, are eligible to become leaders in their own gender-specific domains. At the same time, however, one must never make the mistake of thinking that men and women are interchangeable and the same. They are not. A male leader is naturally and optimally masculine, and is never effeminate. He is either an alpha male or a sigma male, never a beta male. He is strong. He is always kind to his own people, and merciless with the enemies of his people. A female leader is naturally and optimally feminine, and never irascible, manipulative, or lacking in self-control. She must have a strongly inspiring personality. She is nurturing and empathetic toward her people, but is unforgiving toward her people's enemies.

A king and his consort especially must possess these, among many other, positive and complimentary qualities. The king and his consort are the symbolic father and mother of their nation.

2.17 Much of the male population in modern and post-modern Western societies have suffered, either directly or unconsciously, from the debilitating effects of a systematic campaign of devirilization that has been artificially imposed upon them against their will. Through the means of operational propaganda and subtle psychological warfare conducted primarily through the media, entertainment and educational system, otherwise strong and virile men have been bullied into suppressing the natural urge to fully express their organic and healthy masculine tendencies. As a direct result of this malevolent campaign of anti-masculinity, many males in modernity have now found themselves experiencing debilitating feelings of emasculation, disempowerment,

and lacking the healthy confidence that their fathers and grandfathers before them intrinsically wielded. Not only have men themselves suffered as a result of this malevolent anti-masculinity agenda, but all of Western society has now suffered due to the absence of strong and effective men and fathers, and thus strong and effective leaders, in our societies. Strong leaders arise from strong men. Where strong men are in short supply, there will necessarily be a lack of true leadership. It is crucial that this deep-rooted damage that has been inflicted upon men now be thoroughly reversed, and that the revirilization of men now occur in all of Western society.

2.18 The leadership class consists of what are often termed alpha males. Alpha males are men who exhibit such personal traits as confidence, assertiveness, fearlessness, strength, resiliency, optimism, energy, self-respect, and responsibility. Anyone who aspires to be a leader should, at a shear minimum, cultivate such alpha male characteristics. Greater and more rare than the alpha male, however, is the sigma male. A sigma male is a man who possesses all of the alpha male traits honed to perfection, but in addition, the sigma male is free of the reckless bravado, narcissism, self-aggrandizement, and boisterous mouthiness that is found in many ordinary alpha males. The alpha male is a wolf; but the sigma male is a lion. The sigma male leader tends to be more quiet, observant, reserved, introspective and serious than

the ordinary alpha male. Their presence in any given situation exudes the quiet power, the majesty, the regality, the weight, and the dignity of the mightiest mountain. The ordinary king may be an alpha male. But the Chakravartin, the ultimate leader, is a sigma male. The sigma male is akin to a silent, yet wholly unopposable, human weapon.

2.19 One can only have true faith in that which is honest and real. It is for this reason that God Himself is the most ideal recipient of our true faith. A true and honest leader is also a worthy recipient of our faith. A real leader does not allow the people to place their faith in him unless he is fully capable of leading with complete honesty, incorruptibility and authenticity of being. It is only in such a leader that we can, and should, have full and true faith.

2.20 There is no such thing as a true leader who is also an unethical or an immoral person. A person can either choose to be a leader or else he can choose to be unethical. He can never choose to be both simultaneously. A leader must be motivated by an inherently good will. He must be ethical in his inner motivations. He must observe a strict sense of morality in his actions. He must view evil behavior, both within himself and in others, as his personal enemy to be fully eradicated.

2.21 When implementing any actions that are predicated upon vital moral concerns, engaging in half measures is the same as engaging no measures at all. To not mete out full and equitable justice against evil is itself an evil injustice. In all important ethical decisions, it is crucial that one do the right thing wholly and without compromise. If one is incapable of doing so, then that person must assign the task immediately to someone who can.

2.22 In the mind of a good leader, the very existential nature of the presence of evil in any person or thing is that it serves the sole purpose of that evil person or thing being annihilated by him. *Vinashaya dushkritam*. Evil exists only to be annihilated, and the perfect and true leader lives to annihilate evil. He never hesitates in eradicating evil.

2.23 Never make the mistake of viewing the sworn enemies of the Good, those who are responsible for creating largescale evil in this world, as being omnipotent in their abilities. The purveyors of evil are neither omnipotent, nor invincible. To falsely see them as such only psychologically debilitates those who are leaders and fighters for good. Such a mistaken view only serves to drain the good of their energy and hope. Rather, take strength in knowing that the overseers of evil in our world are ultimately impotent and defenseless against the power of God and God's people. No matter how powerful the forces of evil may appear, they can be - and will be - defeated. Evil is never omnipotent. The only being who is omnipotent is God.

2.24 Do not mistake a fake leader for a true leader. Career politicians, bureaucrats, technocrats, professional experts and celebrities are not ever to be mistaken for real leaders. A chimpanzee can be dressed in a beautiful royal robe, bedecked with jewels, and placed upon a throne by his handlers. But the moment that a simple banana is tossed onto the ground before it, the chimpanzee will mindlessly jump off the throne, eagerly leaving its royal accouterments and grand paraphernalia to the wayside, and greedily grab the banana. Thus the chimpanzee inevitably displays its true nature for the entire world to see. The fake leader inevitably does so as well.

Adhyaya Three: Leadership in Action

3.1 The nation, properly constituted in perfect alignment with the principles of Dharma, and governed by a true and empowered ruler, is a divine idea in the mind of God. Such a blessed nation is a replication of the Divine Order upon the earth, and serves as the example to other nations of what a Dharma Nation should look like and how it should operate.

3.2 A true leader of a nation needs a dual mandate if he is going to rule in righteousness and with legitimate authority. He needs the Mandate of God and he needs the Mandate of the People. The Mandate of God is provided if, and only if, the ruler is conducting all of his activities in complete accordance with the principles of Dharma, and if he recognizes his role in governing the nation as his humble, personal service toward God. The Mandate of the People is provided if, and only if, the ruler accurately understands, efficiently responds to, and has the enthusiastic support of the vast majority of the people of his nation. The moment that either of these Mandates is withdrawn, then the ruler cannot rule the nation with legitimate authority.

If both Mandates are withdrawn simultaneously, then that ruler has become subverted into an enemy of the nation rather than the protector of the nation.

3.3 There are only a small number of essential duties that the administration of any good leader must perform in regard to the governance of a nation. These essential functions include the following: 1) ruling the nation in full accordance with the philosophical principles of Dharma, 2) ensuring that the citizens of the nation, as well as the leaders of all sectors of society, uphold the principles of Dharma to the best of their ability under all circumstances, 3) ensuring that the ethnic/genetic integrity and purity of the nation is never imperiled or threatened in any way; 4) defending the nation vigorously from all enemies within and without the nation; 5) punishing all criminals, enemies of the people, traitors to the nation, parasitic elements, and corrupt political leaders resolutely, severely and without hesitation in accordance with Dharmic law;

6) representing the nation with dignity, pride, loyalty, and fidelity in all matters of foreign relations, trade negotiations, and diplomacy. While all six of these duties are crucial if the nation is to prosper, it is the fifth duty that is of foundational importance for the principled operation of the nation. This is the case because, it is in punishing criminals, traitors against the people, and corrupt politicians that all the other five duties are automatically supported.

3.4 Freedom is a Dharmic value. Tyranny is a demonic value. A leader in any sector of governance – whether a president, governor, representative, mayor, or any other office holder – must seek always to ensure the maximal degree of decentralization of governmental authority; the maximal degree of localized governmental authority; the maximal reduction of bureaucracy and regulation; and the maximal degree of liberty and freedom for the citizens as is possible within, and not contradictory to, the jurisdictional and ethical principles of Dharma. Government, even under the best of circumstances, tends to be a burden upon all sectors of the population, and not a benefit. Thus, government is best when it is at its very smallest.

3.5 Meritocratic hierarchy is a direct, unalterable and perfect expression of Nature herself. Throughout history, nations have only been successful in direct proportion to the degree to which each specific nation has respected and upheld natural social hierarchical norms. Those nations that respected social hierarchical norms with the greatest firmness have enjoyed the paramount degree of success on every level – cultural, economic, literary, intellectual and spiritual. Those nations, on the other hand, that have misunderstood, disrespected and rejected natural hierarchical norms within their societies have suffered the worst degree of ruination on every level. Such societies inevitably experience such debilitating states as degeneration, corruption, depression and anxiety among the population,

a thoughtless rejection of true and tested traditional values, and the eventual fall of the nation itself at the hands of alien invaders. A true leader thus ensures that his nation uphold the greatest respect for natural meritocratic hierarchy.

3.6 A wise leader understands who all of the powerful individuals, families, groups (both public and hidden), and nations are within his sphere of operation. He understands their intrinsic natures, their motivations, their histories, and he has full knowledge of the exact degree of their power and influence. He thus divides such individual entities into the three categories of 1) allies, 2) enemies, and 3) yet to be determined, or truly neutral. In order to have such clarity of vision of the nature of these entities, and thus having the ability to place each in their proper category, the leader must be an absolute expert in the formulation and implementation of such organizing and strategizing tools of the intellect as discrimination, discernment of essentialism, categorization, compartmentalization, and hierarchy.

3.7 The truly experienced leader knows the enemy of his people better than that enemy knows himself. He understands what are the enemy's motivations, how the enemy thinks, and what the enemy's plans and strategy are. He especially understands very intimately what their weaknesses are and how to trigger those weaknesses if and when such an occurrence should become a necessity. The experienced leader must always, in actuality, have the upper hand against the enemies of his people, even unbeknownst to the enemy.

3.8 The leader understands that the qualities of mercy, loyalty and trust are never to be extended toward those who are evil, but only toward those who are good. He is never naïve in his dealing with his enemy. To extend mercy, loyalty and trust to those who are evil is to actually thoughtlessly punish those who are good. When evil people prosper, good people suffer. Thus, he keeps evil at bay from his people, and allows his people to prosper in safety and peace.

3.9 The experienced leader never suffers from any form of naiveté or gullibility when it comes to understanding the actual nature of his enemy and the enemy of his people. Underestimating the full extent and depths that evil is capable of descending to leads to the consequent destruction of the good. A leader who makes such a mistake is to be seen as weak and effeminate, and not as a true leader or even a true man. Such adolescent naiveté on the part of an inexperienced leader has the potential to bring about the severe destruction of his people. However depraved you may think evil people are, understand that in actuality they are probably more evil than what you are capable of presently imagining.

3.10 The experienced leader understands who the true enemy actually is, and not merely the contrived adversary who the enemy seeks to misdirect his attention toward. The experienced leader knows that the enemy is never charitable or well-meaning toward him or his people, but merely seeks to exploit his weakness. The enemy often purposefully appears vulnerable and non-threatening, and seeks to exploit the good-hearted leader's natural empathy. The enemy will cry out in pain as if he were a victim as he simultaneously stabs you in the back. It is for this reason that empathy and compassion are wasted upon the evil-doers (*dushkritam*). The enemy is never truly a benefactor, but is a destructively parasitic element in society who seeks to harm the people via infiltration, corruption, bribery and subversion of every form.

As is true with any harmful parasitic pathogen, the enemy is to be thoroughly expelled from the social body in order to protect the people.

3.11 Never view the enemy as monolithic, as a mighty and undivided wall of strength. They are not. Regardless of how strongly united the enemy may falsely appear, they have very real divisions and factions within their very own ranks. It takes tremendous mental discipline, as well as strategic wisdom and psychological insight, on the part of a good leader to be able to adroitly navigate the divisions among the enemy. The true leader must play that enemy faction that is closest in sympathies with his own position against that faction that is furthest away – and which is thus a deadlier enemy – to his own people's interests. The supposed monolithic nature of the enemy is no more than an empty illusion. Break it.

3.12 The deadliest enemy is the one who has placed himself closest to you. He is the one who has deliberately put himself in a place of trust in your eyes. Under all circumstances, always be supremely aware of the surreptitious presence of the enemy within your midst. Always strive to uncover who the true enemy are, where they are, and what they are doing at any given moment. But never allow them to know that you are aware of their presence…until you are ready to let them know under your own terms, and decisively so.

3.13 The enemy at the gates is the external, and thus the more overtly obvious, enemy. This obvious enemy is to be defeated decisively and without hesitation. More deadly that the obvious enemy, however, is the enemy who lies within one's own gates, within one's own society. This enemy will imitate you in every way, looking and sounding like you, exploiting your own recognized cultural norms and social behavior as a cover for his duplicitous and traitorous schemes. He undermines you through seeming familiarity. But, even while pretending to be just like you, he will all the while be secretly working toward your demise. Like a poisonous weed, such an enemy must never be allowed to take root in your society. The enemy within is potentially much more dangerous that the enemy without.

3.14 Whenever a good and virtuous person is attacked by enemy detractors, such cowardly attacks only make the good person stronger, wiser, more agile in combatting the enemy, and more determined to achieve total victory. More, once their duplicitous campaign of smearing and trolling has been exposed to the people, the enemy will eventually be exposed as duplicitous liars in the eyes of the public. In this way, the more the enemy detractors attack the good person, the more they are actually doing him a favor – and ensuring their own inevitable destruction at his hands.

3.15 A corrupt and inept leader often instills a debilitating fear of imaginary enemies within the minds of the populace of his nation. He either invents false enemies, or else he deflects against those who are not enemies at all, concealing the true enemies who his people should resist. He does this with the aim of dishonestly controlling the people through their fear. He cynically attempts to brainwash his people through contrived propaganda, rather than share factual information about the true enemy with his people. All the while, the true enemy silently grows in power and strength. In this way, the corrupt leader is himself an enemy of his people. A true national leader, instead, encourages vigilance in the hearts of his people against the confirmed enemies of the nation. Rather than scheming to control his people via their fear,

a true national leader seeks to unleash his people's strength and courage through their vigilance against the actual enemies of the nation. It is only when the identity of the true enemy is confirmed and re-vealed that this antagonistic opponent can be defeated.

3.16 A true and able leader of his people is never a globalist, but is always a nationalist. He leads in the exclusive service of his nation and the people of his nation, and not the globe as a whole. A truly intelligent leader knows that success and victory do not revolve around the artificially imposed unanimity of all global peoples, and that any such forced integration only leads to tyranny and the degeneration of all human societies. The true leader is not the ruler of all peoples or of the entire world. Rather, he understands that success and victory involve only unity among his own, specific and homogeneous people.

3.17 An honest leader is the leader of his own people, his own ethnos, the uniquely indigenous folk population of his nation who share his ancestral and genetic heritage. In establishing the unity of his own irreplaceable people, the leader has now organized one of the most formidable social-political forces available to him – the nation. But the moment that he sees himself as a leader of the globe, rather than a leader of his own unique people, he ceases to be his people's friend and is now their enemy. Globalists are, by definition, enemies of their own people. Globalists are to be always opposed and defeated by all virtuous and righteous people.

3.18 An intelligent leader must have the ability to work with likeminded people even if such persons are not in complete agreement with all of his views. A leader working with someone who is not in complete agreement with him does not mean that the leader necessarily fully accepts everything that the potential ally proclaims or stands for. It only means that the leader is doing his job as a leader in seeking practical working alliances. If a leader constrains himself from forming alliances with others simply due to those others not sharing complete ideological purity with the leader, then that supposed leader is someone who is guaranteed to accomplish nothing of practical value for his people. Thus, he is not really a leader.

3.19 It is important to always plan and strategize in terms of multiplication of desired effects. A leader tries to ensure that several different goals are accomplished with any single causal action, and not that just only one goal is achieved. The multiplication of desired effects saves time and energy, and thus ensures maximal efficiency in achieving the resultant goals. Acting in such a manner as to accomplish multiple goals with one action, the leader is being wise and proficient.

3.20 True power frequently resides not merely in what one says publicly, before the eyes and ears of all, but in the stealth actions that one takes quietly and beyond the purview of the general public. Power is most effectively wielded deeply behind the scenes, not on the public stage. For this reason, the leader must be adroit in the fields of diplomacy, negotiation, intelligence gathering, strategizing and human psychology. The most important achievements are often accomplished in silence.

3.21 Often the most powerful people are those who work in relative obscurity in a capacity of advisory support of the leader. Thus, advisors to the leader are often quite powerful personages in their own right. For this reason, the leader must be very careful in whom he places his trust as potential advisors. A wise leader never allows his advisor to become a center point of power and influence independent of the leader, as this might eventually lead to a dangerous conflict of interests. Only if the advisor has proven himself to be loyal and trustworthy beyond all doubt, and for a very long duration of time, should the leader fully trust the advisor.

3.22 Politics in not defined merely by the sharing of one's opinions, but that the practical activities necessary to acquire and wield power. The definition of politics is twofold: a) those aspects of the political struggle that are used to achieve the acquisition of power previous to accomplishing political success, and b) those policies that will be implemented via governance upon the eventual acquisition of political power. A wise leader understands that these two aspects of politics are very different from one another, and are necessarily sequential fields of political endeavor. What one does in order to acquire political power is not the same as what one does in the implementation of policy once power is obtained. The wise leader does not confuse one of these for the other.

3.23 A political leader understands that there are four distinct components of a political movement. These four components are: a) the ideological element, b) strategy, c) propaganda and messaging, and finally d) policy and governance. Ideology is the philosophical foundation and vision-oriented component of one's political stance. Strategy is the systematic plan by which one intends to attain real-world political power. Propaganda and messaging are the persuasive narratives that one will give the people in order to gain their support and loyalty. Policy and governance can only be implemented once one has attained actual political power, and is thus in possession of the institutional tools necessary to affect legislative and executive change. It is crucial to keep these four elements separate in one's mind when engaging in political struggle,

and to not confuse one for the other. It is often be-cause activists confuse one of these elements for the other that political movements end up disas-trously failing.

3.24 Ethics pertain to all areas of politics. The following comports with the nature of ethics specifically in the realm of ideology. For people who are evil, ideology serves as a mere means of acquiring power. The realm of ideas for such unethical politicians is nothing more than a mere tool used in fooling the people to support such unethical politicians in their selfish pursuit of personal power. For good people, on the other hand, power is a means for implementing a positive, ethically rooted ideology. Power, for such ethical people, exists merely in order to serve the ideal. A true leader always serves the ideal above any personal political ambition.

3.25 One of the primary duties of every political leader, whether on the local or national level, is the defense of the community, the nation and the people of the nation. Every other consideration, issue and policy is secondary to the defense of the nation. The defense of the nation means not only defending the nation militarily from obvious external enemies, but also preserving the religion, culture, values, historical and ancestral heritage, and ethnic integrity of the nation. Thus, the nation must be steadfastly defended from both external and internal enemies.

3.26 Innocence is one of the most important human qualities that society requires in order to remain truly civilized. Innocence is sacred. Innocence must be cherished and preserved with as much vigilance as would be given to the safety of the nation's wealth, the nation's leader, or the nation's borders. The leader is the protector of innocence, as are all righteous warriors. Wherever he encounters an innocent person, especially innocent women and children, he spares no personal expense in protecting such exemplary people against evil and exploitation, even to the point of sacrificing his own life if necessary. In giving his life in the defense of innocence, the virtuous leader assures his place in the heavens.

Additionally, those evil individuals who are responsible for harming or exploiting the innocent must be afforded zero mercy, and must be punished to the maximal degree.

3.27 Under no circumstances should a city ever be allowed to have more than 50,000 citizens. When ruled by enlightened and Dharmic leadership, such a city can be a beautifully sattvic (i.e., of the nature of purity, goodness, health, and refinement) territory. When ruled by common leadership, on the other hand, the city will be highly influenced by *rajas* (i.e., uncontrolled passion). When the population is allowed to go significantly above 50,000 people, the city soon descends into the darkness of *tamas* (i.e., ignorance, darkness and degeneracy). The direct result of a city descending into such darkness is that corruption, crime, lawlessness, vice, pollution, stress and anxiety, ugliness, and materialism will all thrive in the city.

3.28 A true leader keeps the city's population from ever going above 50,000 people and ensures that the city's culture is sattvic in nature. Any city that currently has a population that is significantly above this number should immediately undergo the systematic and gradual reduction of its population until the goal of having less than 50,000 citizens is achieved. Rather than directing resources to rancid urban areas, a maximal amount of resources must be redirected to the much more wholesome rural sectors in order to ensure that these rural areas are sustained and encouraged to thrive and prosper. Under the able guidance of a good city leader, every current city must meet the goal of having a population of under 50,000 people.

3.29 One of the most important tasks of the political leader is to ensure that the nation, state, city, village, or sector that he is in charge of cultivates and celebrates beauty in all its many forms. The layout of the city must be arranged in such a manner as to be pleasing to the gods and to the citizens. Virtuous artists in every field of aesthetic endeavor must be supported and encouraged by the state to create works of beauty that reflect the eternal laws of nature, the blessings of the gods, the will of God, and the spirit of the People of the nation and their revered ancestors. Music, dance and theater that reflect the highest spiritual virtues of Dharma must be present throughout every aspect of society. Language itself must be purified of all debased words and expressions, brought to the maximal heights of poetic expression,

and verbally uttered in a beautiful manner by the People. Gardens filled with aromatic flowers and pleasingly scented plants should be established throughout every city, town and village. Beauty in the visual appearance of individual persons must be socially encouraged and celebrated, and all ugliness must be comprehensively shunned. The citizens should be encouraged to keep physically fit, healthy, and to be both dignified and proud in their personal appearance at all times.

3.30 A true leader always makes certain that the basic needs of his followers are well taken care of, regardless of the organizational sector of society that he is leading. A spiritual leader serves his followers by making sure that he lives an exemplary life, and follows the religious principles that he is teaching even better than any of his followers. In this way, he takes care of his followers by providing a vivid example that they can emulate. A political leader makes sure that the basic needs of all the citizens are met at all times. A military general makes sure that his men are well-fed, well-trained, and provided for medically. A business owner makes sure that his employees are not being exploited or abused. A leader must be responsive to the concerns and needs of his people always.

3.31 A good leader corrects the arrogance and disobedience of his inferiors swiftly and decisively. He quickly puts fools in their place with detachment and dispassion. If he does not do so, then the fools among his subordinates will potentially reach positions of power that they were never qualified or organically destined to occupy. Such a qualitative inversion of meritocratic hierarchy would be guaranteed to bring direct suffering to the people, because unqualified leaders bring nothing but distress to those who they are supposed to be leading. A true and capable leader never allows such an unnatural inversion of meritocratic hierarchy to ever occur.

3.32 It is, unfortunately, too often through reactionary emotional appeals and succumbing to petty self-interests that the masses are moved to action. Demonic and corrupt politicians fully understand this fact of social psychology and use this knowledge to manipulate the masses toward anti-Dharmic goals. The true and legitimate leader, on the other hand, is himself only ever moved to action by logical thinking; a strong desire to serve the actual interests of the people; and the formulation of patient, long-term strategies. In this way, the true leader does not assuage the transient emotions of the masses, but leads the masses toward their own higher interests. A true leader does not answer to the emotional impulses of the masses; but to the true needs of his citizens. A true leader does not manipulate; he inspires.

3.33 The ideal leader is to provide Truth and Justice for his people. Truth prevails only when one's thinking is devoid of faulty predispositions that are based upon ephemeral emotions. One must fully understand and practice the principles of Dharma in order to guarantee clear and sharp thinking, and thus direct access to Truth. Justice is ensured only by practicing self-disciplined gravitas while engaging in calm and patient deliberation. Self-disciplined gravitas is achieved through the daily, steadfast practice of Yoga and meditation. We serve Truth and Justice best when we view the world through the eyes of God.

Adhyaya Four: Leadership in the Five Psycho-physical Classes

4.1 To those accustomed to mediocrity, the ideal of excellence feels like oppression.

4.2 There are five distinct psychophysical categories (*varna*) of human beings, who are accordingly classified into five corresponding classes. These five psychophysical classes are the *brahmanas* (intellectual-priestly class), the *kshatriyas* (warrior-administrative class), the *vaishyas* (farmer-mercantile, producer class), the *shudras* (laborer-craftsman class), and the *chandalas* (the delinquent-degraded, barbaric class). The first four are accepted within Vedic society. The fifth is not, and is kept at a far distance from the citizens of a Vedic state in order to ensure their safety and purity. All of these distinct classes have leaders within their respective communities that correspond with the particular natures of their communities.

4.3 A *brahmana* is the spiritual leader of society. He is sattvic by nature. Among the *brahmanas*, those individuals are accepted as leaders who possess the inherent attributes of intelligence, philosophical acumen, cleanliness, purity, spirituality, consistency, discipline, focus, the ability to teach, inner peace and tranquility, unyielding fidelity to tradition, self-realization, devotion toward God, and unbreakable adherence to Dharma, among other indispensable qualities. The *brahmana* is, by definition, one who knows Brahman (God).

4.4 *Kshatriyas* are the political and martial leaders of society. Among the *kshatriyas*, those people are accepted as leaders who have the inherent characteristics of courage, strength, discipline, focus, spirituality, consistency, sharp senses, physical prowess, fortitude, endurance, charisma, administrative ability, strategic foresight, political intuition, steadiness, devotion to the *brahmanas*, and full adherence to Dharma, among other qualities. The definition of a *kshatriya* is one who is a Dharma Warrior.

4.5 Leaders of the *vaishya* community share the following characteristics: an innovative mind, risk-
taking, ingenuity, excellent negotiation skills, a charitable disposition, creativity, enthusiasm, piety,
confidence and faith in Vedic civilization, among
other qualities. *Vaishyas* create the wealth of society,
most especially in the form of agricultural produce.
They are always subservient to the *brahmanas* and
the *kshatriyas*. But they serve all of society in as
much as they provide the very nutritional suste-
nance that all sectors of society need in order to
thrive. *Vaishyas* are, by definition, creators of wealth
and produce.

4.6 *Shudra* leaders have a strong camaraderie with their fellow workers, an amiable personality, a service attitude, as well as finely-honed skills in their own craft. *Shudra* leaders often supervise trade guilds. A truly honorable *shudra* understands that it is not enough merely to do his job. Rather, he must do his job well. He seeks excellence in his craftmanship. *Shudra* leaders always inspire their followers to do their utmost to serve the greater interests of society, and to be subservient to the *brahmanas*, *kshatriyas* and *vaishyas*. By definition, a *shudra* is someone who takes pride in his works hard, loyalty and dependability.

4.7 *Chandala* leaders agitate, rabble rouse and cynically manipulate their followers into destructive action. They appeal to emotion over reason, selfish self-interest over idealism, envy over honor, and violence over debate. Rather than encourage their followers to work hard to honestly earn successes in life, *chandala* leaders encourage their followers to loot, riot and steal from those people who form the productive sector of society. *Chandala* leaders have no personal sense of ethics, discipline, honor or compassion. They are the blind leading the blind. Marxist agitators are a prime contemporary example of *chandala* leaders in action. *Chandala* leaders are enemies of Dharma and of the People, and are to be treated as a dangerous alien element within society. *Chandalas* are, by definition, envious and parasitic in their nature.

4.8 The first four of these classes are considered to be the naturally occurring classes that are found among the population of *manushya*, or proper humans persons. The last of these classes - *chandalas* - are understood to fall within the category of *amanushya*, or sub-humans. Human and sub-human living entities, cultures, or modes of behavior can never be reconciled or integrated into human society, but are to be at all times kept apart from civilization by the greatest degree of separation for the ultimate well-being of all humanity. Only humans (*manushya*) have the potential capacity of exhibiting *arya* (noble) behavior. Sub-humans (*amanushya*), by contrast, are habitually capable of only exhibiting *anarya* (ignoble) behavior.

It is for this reason that the true leader never allows the *amanushya* to ever have access to, or to intermix with, the *manushya* under his protection.

4.9 While there is often a genetic-inheritance factor operative in the determination of which of these five classes a specific individual should be situated in, one's parentage in and of itself is insufficient for making such a determination. Both nature and nurture can be trumped by the factor of will. By the power of one's will, for example, one can have been born from *shudra* parents, and yet still be a *brahmana* in one's own personal nature (*svadharma*). Thus, the category that one's parents are in is not necessarily determinative of the category that the individual belongs to. There is always room for fluidity in the Vedic *varna* (psychophysical class) system.

4.10 By the incomparable grace of God, coupled with the person's unyielding determination, even a *shudra* can potentially someday become a *brahmana*. By the devious power of illusion, even a *brahmana* may eventually fall down to the level of a *shudra*. Free-will trumps both nature and nurture.

4.11 There are four primary forms of intelligence. These four are, in qualitatively descending order: 1) wisdom, 2) factual intelligence, 3) sub-discursive thought, and 4) manipulative cunning. It is in understanding the respective natures of each of these four intelligences, as well as the stark distinctions between them all, that the able leader can grasp both the intrinsic nature and capabilities of all those whom he encounters.

4.12 Wisdom is knowledge (*jnana*) that is of the nature of the eternal, transcendent, pure and good. Such wisdom is acquired by directly accessing one's innate *buddhi*, or wisdom-faculty, which is an inherent power of the soul (*atman*) itself. Wisdom is, thus, reflective of the nature of pure consciousness. Wisdom is not relative, subjective or conditional. The contents of wisdom are perpetual throughout time, and are not subject to essential modification.

4.13 Factual intelligence is knowledge that is derived primarily from empirical observation, coupled with a grasp of quantitative facts and data. Factual intelligence is derived from the human person's material intellectual faculty. Scientists and many academics employ factual intelligence in their professions.

4.14 Sub-discursive thought is knowledge that is derived, not from discursive or conscious thought, but primarily from perceptive data impressed upon the senses and/or which agitate the emotions. Sub-discursive thought is reactionary in its nature and function. The localized realm of sub-discursive thought is within the lower echelons of the mental sphere (*manas*) and in the emotions (*abhitapa*).

4.15 Manipulative cunning is in many ways the very opposite of the above three, and consists of an innate ability to warp both perception and thought-content exclusively toward one's self-serving and rapacious advantage. Manipulative cunning is fully sourced in, and dependent upon, illusion (*maya*, or "that which is not"). Manipulative cunning is the thought process employed by narcissists, psychopaths, sadists, grifters and con-artists, and by parasitic individuals.

4.16 Authentic *brahmanas* operate primarily through wisdom. The thought processes of *brahmanas* are centered upon axiomatic principles that are necessarily and eternally true. *Kshatriyas* employ a mixture of wisdom and factual intelligence. *Vaishyas* use a mixture of factual intelligence, with a limited degree of manipulative cunning. *Shudras* engage primarily in sub-discursive thought. *Chandalas* employ a mixture of sub-discursive thought and manipulative cunning. *Asuras* (demonic psychopaths) use primarily manipulative cunning. There is sometimes a degree of overlap in the forms of intelligences that the different classes will employ. The *brahmanas*, however, are the only people who can successfully use all four forms of intelligence, as a particular circumstance may warrant, and always exclusively in the service and defense of Dharma.

4.17 Of all the classes (*varnas*), it is specifically the *brahmana* class and the *kshatriya* class that are considered to be the leadership classes over all others. It is the *brahmanas* (operating in the field of religion and spirituality) and the *kshatriyas* (operating in the fields of politics and the military) who bear the responsibility of leading the rest of society. The *kshatriyas* respect the wise counsel of their *brahmana* advisors; and the *brahmanas* respect the role of the *kshatriyas* as society's natural temporal rulers. It is for this reason that the *brahmanas* and *kshatriyas* must always work very closely together as the dual natural leadership classes of society in order to ensure that the Vedic community operates in a uncontaminated, peaceful, well-ordered and prosperous way for the benefit of all the citizens.

4.18 The vast majority of individuals fall into either one or another of the above five classes (the four *varnas*, and the *chandalas*, who are considered to be a sub-*varna*). There is, however, an additional class that is considered to be superior to all the above classes. The highest and purest of *varnas* (classes) is the rarely encountered *vajra-varna* (the Thunderbolt class, alternately known as the Diamond class). Those of the *vajra-varna* display the qualities of the *brahmana* and the *kshatriya* in equal portions, in a seamlessly harmonious integration, and to a wholly maximal degree. Such a person is, at one and the same time, both a perfect sage, and a perfect warrior. He is a seer-monarch, a warrior-priest, a god-emperor, a regal-ascetic, and a philosopher-king. It is from the ranks of the *vajra-varna* that

the Chakravartins (godly-kings, literally "Wielders of the Wheel of Dharma") are born. In the Kali Yuga, especially, it is those of the *vajra-varna* who have repeatedly saved Dharma throughout the history of the world.

Adhyaya Five: The Ultimate Leader

5.1 The ultimate leader (*parama-nayaka*) is uniquely situated above all other leaders because of two factors: a) his essence is non-different from his people and from his given mission; and b) because his essence is wholly incorruptible. Thus, in both of these factors, it is the essential nature of the ultimate leader that sets him apart from others. The ultimate leader is possessed of these two qualities precisely because his vision of reality is free from all illusion and self-interest. Thus, he is someone who stands outside of the normative perceptions and motivations displayed by the vast majority of people.

He is not motivated by a personal need for power, or by greed, or by the desire for fame and adoration. His motivations are completely selfless in that they are focused upon the needs of those whom he leads. In this way, the ultimate leader is unique in his internal, essential being, and he is radically superior to other leaders.

5.2 An ultimate leader's essence is non-distinct from his people and his mission in that he is invested in his people and in his mission with all of his thoughts, words and actions. His role as a leader is not merely a job or a career to him; rather, it is his deepest calling. It is familial love for his people, and the strong desire to ensure his people's future survival, that motivate him internally. His people constitute his spiritual and ancestral roots, his ethnic and genetic heritage, and his extended family. He will live, and if necessary die, for the protection and betterment of his people. It is the ultimate leader's love of his people that fuels his unyielding focus upon his given mission. It is his single-minded dedication to his mission that is his sole calling in this world, and that propels him on all levels of his being, and at every moment of his life.

The well-being of his people and the completion of his mission constitute the very essential being of the ultimate leader.

5.3 The overwhelming majority of common folk are prone to eventual corruption in direct proportion to the amount of power placed within the purview of their control. The more power a person or group of persons possess, the greater is the probability of corruption on the part of those persons. Not all persons, however, are corruptible. This is the case because not all persons are exactly the same, or in any way equal. There is an extremely small number of people who are, in fact, not prone to corruption at all. They are, indeed, incorruptible. Their agency is wholly pure. The ultimate leader is one such representative of this small number of incorruptible agents.

5.4 The ultimate leader (*parama-nayaka*) is in all ways absolutely incorruptible. The ultimate leader is incorruptible in that his will and motivations are based upon his innately good virtue, and not upon the crass concerns of material acquisition that motivate the common person. His innate virtue being wholly good, consequently his will and motivations are also wholly good. He is incapable of being corrupted by any of the temptations of the material world. His reaction to the sight of gold is as his reaction would be to the sight of dirt. Thus, he exhibits good conduct in all of his accomplishments.

5.5 Power does, indeed, corrupt those who are in-herently prone to corruption. Absolute power does, likewise, corrupt absolutely those who are, by dint of their subjugation to illusion and ignorance, nec-essarily prone to corruption. But absolute power is the obedient servant of that ultimate leader who is surrendered wholly to the Absolute, who has liber-ated himself completely from all material illusion, and who thus renders himself incapable of any worldly corruption. It is only in being wholly sur-rendered to the Absolute that an enlightened leader can wield absolute power without the possibility of corruption.

5.6 The two inherent qualities of the ultimate leader are that his essence is non-distinct from his people, and he is inherently incorruptible. The ultimate leader is born with these two inherent qualities that have been thus far elaborated upon in the previous aphorisms. These qualities are with him at the very time of his birth. These inherent qualities cannot merely be learned by someone who is not born with them, but only imitated. This being said, however, even though these inherent qualities are inborn within him, even the ultimate leader must often have these intrinsic qualities drawn out of him over time by an expert guide and *guru*. Even a born leader must seek to cultivate his inward qualities of leadership through the acquisition of wisdom, inner strength and spiritual attainment.

5.7 The ultimate leader lives much of his life –
even his childhood - as someone who inwardly
stands apart and distinct from the bulk of the
masses. He is inherently unlike most of the people
who surround him. He is the outsider, the outlier,
the person whose nature is both unique and qualitatively above those around him. Throughout his life
- beginning even when he was a child - his personal
interests, natural predilections, cherished values, innate goals, and unique personality are very different
from the majority of other people in society. He is
what is termed an outsider, a radically distinct personality who is more concerned with being faithful
to what is real, true and meaningful than appealing
to popularity. For this reason, he is often misunderstood in his youth, and sometimes even
intimidating to others.

He is someone who is not interested in making small-talk with others, but only in making big-talk. The ultimate leader begins his public life as someone who seemingly stands outside of the normative concerns of his society because his vision is exceedingly expansive. It is due to the fact that he is spiritually situated above his people that he can most perfectly instantiate the very spirit of his people.

5.8 The three types of *parama-nayakas* (ultimate leaders) are: a) spiritual, b) political, and c) a perfectly wedded combination of both. The first is called a Jagad Guru, a "World Teacher". The status and accomplishments of the Jagad Guru are beyond that of a spiritual teacher in the normative sense. In addition to fulfilling the roll of a spiritual teacher, the Jagad Guru is a *guru* who also establishes Dharma in a way that is conspicuously world-changing in effect. Such Jagad Gurus have included Narada Muni, Vyasa, Gautama Buddha, Ramanuja-Acharya, and Prabhupada, among others. The second type of leader operates primarily in the political sphere in such a manner that he ensures the safety and prosperity of his people and alters the course of history for the better, and in accordance with Dharmic principles. He is not a sage per se, but he

has spirituality as an exceedingly important foundation of his being. There have been hundreds of examples of such specifically political leaders historically. The third type of leader is called a Chakravartin, a "Wielder of the Wheel of Dharma". A Chakravartin reconciles in his innate being the very best qualities of both the spiritual and political *parama-nayakas* (ultimate leaders). He is a perfect sage and a perfect ruler. Such Chakravartins have included Sri Rama, Rishabha, Yudhishthira, Huangdi, Shakyamuni Buddha, and King Arthur, among others. The Chakravartin is a human manifestation of Dharma upon the Earth as Dharma is expressed in both the spiritual and temporal domains of concern. All three types of ultimate leaders have Dharma and the spiritual as the solid basis of all their thoughts, words and actions.

5.9 There are three leadership styles that leaders employ in relation to their followers. Some leaders lead from a place that is situated far above their people. Theirs is the way of inspiration, awe and majesty. Others lead from within the very midst of their people. They exhibit the qualities of personal example and the love of camaraderie with the common folk. They are on the front lines with their people. The ultimate leader, however, leads his people perfectly in both of these manners, from above and from within their midst. His people are in awe and reverence of him, and simultaneously love him dearly as their premier comrade.

5.10 The most perfect form of government for our era, in accordance with Vedic political science, is a constitutional monarchy. A constitutional monarchy ensures that the natural rights of the people are protected by a standard set of recognized legal principles governing the operation and legislative norms of the nation. It simultaneously ensures that there is a strong, multi-generational executive branch of the government that is reflective of the ultimate authority of God and Dharma via the person of the king and the royal family. In a constitutional monarchy, the king is expected to also be subject to the constitution, as are his people. Only a constitutional monarchy can ensure that the nation veers away from the two destructive extremes of tyranny on the one hand,

versus the direct democratic anarchy of the mob on the other hand. A constitutional monarchy is thus the most natural, balanced and just approach to governance.

5.11 God provides His atmic children with the maximal amount of freedom expressible within their individual inherent natures, while also providing the necessary bounds and restrictions that must be present in order to ensure their maximal safety in the exercise of that intrinsic freedom. The true leader does not rule over his people in a totalitarian, authoritarian or tyrannical way; he does not need to. The leader of a nation strives to provide as much meaningful freedom to his people as is possible, both for the individual persons within his kingdom, as well as for the people as a greater whole. The leader's parameters to ensure his people's freedom include the observance of such policies as decentralization of power, the unobtrusiveness of governmental presence, and the absolutely lowest tax burden upon the people

possible (with no tax burden at all being the optimal ideal), and the protection of the people from all elements of crime and threats from the nation's enemies. Simultaneously, the leader also fully expects and requires that the people will, in turn, observe all of the laws, principles and duties decreed upon them by the natural law principles of Dharma as upheld by the nation's constitution and king.

5.12 The more noble, virtuous, inherently intelligent (i.e., in possession of a high IQ) - and thus qualitatively superior - any given population is, the less intrusive, burdensome and heavy-handed government needs to be toward such citizens. Indeed, in a purely Dharmic society, there would barely be the need for any government at all. When, on the other hand, the population is dominated by qualitatively inferior persons, the governing structure tends to be predominantly large, bureaucratic, socialistic, and thus hopelessly corrupt. It is for this reason that traditionally Dharmic societies are ruled by governments that are nearly imperceptible and unobtrusive in their operation. Modern, multicultural nation-states, on the other hand, lean toward overly intrusive, totalitarian government.

The leader of a noble society should work toward creating a government that is nearly invisible to the people.

5.13 The paramount goal of the ultimate leader is to save the world through the instantiation of Dharma in every echelon of society. He wishes to transform the world fundamentally and for the better, down to even every single blade of grass. There is no force in all of creation, aside from his own death, that will deter the ultimate leader from achieving his goal of saving the world. In his determination to fulfill his mission of saving the world, the ultimate leader possesses a will as strong as titanium. There is nothing that can stop the victory of Dharma. Nothing.

5.14 Upon the final completion of all of his earthly tasks, having successfully secured the happiness and wellbeing of the people, and having established Dharma on the strongest of footings within the domain of his kingdom, the ultimate leader then resigns all earthly duties and devotes the remainder of his life to spiritual liberation (*moksha*). Having completed his worldly duties, he now seeks perfection in transcendence.

5.15 Thus ends the guiding *sutra* textbook and manual for true leaders known as the *Principles of Perfect Leadership.* It is in perfectly understanding and living the teachings of this work, under the able guidance of an authentic *guru*, that the true leader will make manifest for the world to witness his inherent nature as a leader of his people.

About the Author

Sri Dharma Pravartaka Acharya is universally acclaimed as one of the world's most respected and qualified Vedic teachers and spiritual leaders of the tradition of Sanatana Dharma. Dr. Deepak Chopra exclaimed in 2002: "*You've done truly phenomenal work teaching the pure essence of Yoga*". In a similar manner, Dr. David Frawley has said about Sri Acharyaji, "*Sri Acharyaji represents the Sankalpa [the will] of the Hindu people and the cause of Sanatana Dharma. I urge all Hindus everywhere to give him your full support, assistance, and encouragement in his crucial work. He needs and deserves our help.*" Indeed, *Hinduism Today Magazine* has proclaimed him one of the top five scholars of Hinduism on earth.

Sri Acharyaji began his personal spiritual journey over 45 years ago at the tender age of ten when he read the *Bhagavad Gita* for the very first time. It was soon thereafter that he began his rigorous practice of Yoga, meditation, *pranayama* and many other ancient Vedic techniques of spiritual awakening.

At approximately twelve years old, he took Yoga lessons from Sri Dharma Mittra and Sri Swami Bua in New York City. Only a few short years later, he took on the lifestyle of a fulltime Vedic monk, living a life of celibacy and great austerity for close to eight years in that capacity. This monastic training culminated in Sri Acharyaji being awarded the status of *brahmana* (Vedic priest) by his *guru*, B.R. Sridhara Swami, in 1986 at his *guru's ashrama* in India.

He coupled his decades of intense spiritual practice and study with advanced academic achievements, earning a B.A. in philosophy/theology from Loyola University Chicago, as well as an M.A. and Ph.D. in religious studies from the University of Wisconsin-Madison. His entire university career was funded by academic fellowships awarded to him as a result of his scholastic excellence and brilliance.

Explaining to his doctoral advisor in 1995 that "*I don't want to just study the history of religion...I want to make religious history*", Sri Acharyaji left academia upon achieving his Ph.D. to devote himself exclusively to spiritual teaching and to the restoration of the great tradition of Sanatana Dharma.

Sri Acharyaji occupies his full time teaching Dharma spirituality to diverse audiences. In addition to leading classes, *satsanghas*, seminars and lecturing on Sanatana Dharma widely, Sri Acharyaji is a renowned author of over ten authoritative books, as well as a personal spiritual guide (*guru*) to a rapidly increasing following of many thousands of enthusiastic students from both the Indian and the non-Indian communities. Currently, he has students and followers in over 80 nations.

Sri Acharyaji was the Resident Acharya (Spiritual Preceptor) of the Hindu Temple of Nebraska from 2007-2009, which represents the first time in American history that a Hindu temple has ever made such an esteemed appointment. Sri Acharyaji is considered by many contemporary *gurus* and leaders

of the Vedic community to be the most cutting-edge, authentic, traditionalist and highly qualified Vedic *guru* in the world today.

Members of the International Sanatana Dharma Society acknowledge Sri Acharyaji as a truly enlightened sage, as a *sad-guru* (true *guru*) capable of guiding his disciples to the deepest realization of wisdom and spiritual liberation, and all members strive to follow his spiritual teachings in our daily lives with sincerity, loyalty and fidelity.

For more information about the life and teachings of Sri Dharma Pravartaka Acharya, please visit his website:

www.dharmacentral.com

Further Information

For more information on this or our other publications by Sri Dharma Pravartaka Acharya, please visit:

Dharmacentral.com

Dharma Central
www.dharmacentral.com
Authentic Spirituality for Today's World

Made in the USA
Coppell, TX
14 July 2022